His B.A.
Was Only $8k:

Quick, Fun, College For Ages 12 to 99

by Kathy Cooksey

Table of Contents

Our Story

Micah I and our sardine-packed family turned out of our driveway, and before we reached a new block passed a shack, a hospital, an apartment complex, and a three-story home. On another routine trip to Tokyo, we rode under digital traffic updates, deciding to take the Tomei Highway rather than the Meishin.

"Can you turn up the video?"
"Can we stop at Starbucks today? Look, an American!"
"Twenty dollars in tolls today."

We found Temple University, and I took him up for his test. The other student testing felt strange that he was 50 years old because Micah was two feet shorter than he was.

The Cookseys had embarked upon unchartered territory. Were they crazy? Micah was 12 years old and had not studied for his test. **But at the end of the day, he had six hours of college credit. Two classes finished.**

Chapter 1: Sorting Out the Mayhem

A run-through of all the questions and their answers

Are The Cookseys Crazy?

That is definitely debatable. But at the time of writing, Micah is 21 years old, has an accredited Bachelor of Arts in Social Sciences and has completed his Master of Arts in Theological Studies online from Midwestern Baptist Theological Seminary. All this was done without debt on a pastor's salary, and Micah paid for his own master's degree.

Taped Glasses and a Sliderule?

No, Micah is a normal guy. (Well, you might want to check with his sisters on that.) He's pretty smart but not a genius, and he would be the first to tell you that almost anyone can do this.

How Did You Do This for So Little Money?

You just have to think outside the box. Micah basically tested out of each college class he needed for his Bachelor's degree.

The first test (when he was 12) was called Analyzing and Interpreting Literature. He passed by one point without studying. Not wanting to cut it that close next time, when 3 of his younger siblings took it, they prepared by reading lots of classic literature beforehand. We found that studying helps with test scores! Others would have realized that in the beginning, but we are a little slow ... So hey, if we can get this done, so can you.

Micah had familiarized himself with the King James Bible, so his mind was ready to read the short passages on the test (the Analyzing and Interpreting Literature CLEP test) and answer the questions about each passage.

The point is, if you're only paying for a test rather than paying for an entire class, you're going to save a LOT of money.

My Age is Closer to the 50-Year-Old Guy in the Story. Is it Too Late for Me?

Absolutely not! *This way of doing college is ideal for older students because the scheduling is flexible, the cost is a fraction of the traditional method, you can learn from home or work, and it is the fast track to finishing.*

Are You By Chance a Weird Religious Zealot Who Doesn't Think that Marxist College Professors Should Enlighten Students?

As a matter of fact, I am! But even if you and I do not share spiritual or political views, you can still benefit from this method of education.

How Did Micah Start When He was Twelve? Did He Forfeit His Fun Teenage Years for Academia?

Actually, he probably spent less time than an average teenager studying at times. So much of college is just a repeat of high school, so since we educate our kids at home, Micah was able to complete high school simultaneously with college!

Do Your Kids Really Learn Anything Doing College This Way?

Oh, they have learned so so very much. All about the Middle East, Russian history, English, Art, Geriatrics, such interesting stuff! I wish I had time to learn all of it myself.

Wait a Minute ~ Skip High School? That *Is* Crazy.

Well, we didn't really skip it.

I knew that so much of high school and college was just repeat material. I knew that elementary-level homeschooled kids who got interested in exciting history books already knew more than I'd ever learned in high school history, and that goes for many other subjects as well. So, I decided that since Micah was so excited about getting going on the college tests that if there was something we missed by basically skipping high school, it would show up in his college studies as a hole or gap, and we could deal with it then. But so far we haven't found any holes at all.

(Please pick yourself up from off of the floor and use an oxygen mask if necessary. I promise this is possible, and my kids have received **an incredible education!**)

What about Painting Couches?

Through this method of education (and through home schooling), my kids have gotten excited about learning. Now when they want to learn something that I never got around to teaching them, they research it for themselves and go for it. They certainly didn't learn from ME how to:

work on a car
paint a couch
make ugly furniture look cool
mount ski boots to a snow board
make their own frames for glasses
make a built-in computer desk with no supports
fix the internet reception in the living room

I realize that most of you don't even *want* your kids painting your couch. And I promise my son Matt is going to wear a helmet if he tries to go down a mountain on his snow board with ski boots on it. But this homeschool journey has created kids who are not afraid of learning.

Is There Any Sort of Company That Could Help Us Weave Through This Confusing Maze of Thinking Outside the Box?

There is an organization called College Plus that helped us get started. They helped us figure out our degree plan, told us which tests to take and how to study, and gave weekly coaching calls.

After the first year, we considered doing this crazy adventure all on our own without College Plus. One major factor to ponder was that we were completely out of money! There are some advantages to being broke all the time – it helps in making decisions.

We did find the rest of the way; except for the (figurative) heart attacks I always suffered wondering if this was really going to work. (Don't worry; it did!!) We couldn't have done it without the wonderful help of our brilliant friend, Julie the Researcher.

College Plus is expensive. In fact, the cost has maybe quadrupled since we paid for College Plus, and I only say that because I don't know the word for quintupled. Quintiplied. Quinpolated. Anyway.

And since we were a part of College Plus, they have seemed to add quite a bit of extra requirements that don't seem necessary to me. Toward the end of our experience, we received the study skills materials. For us, they gathered dust. Maybe they would be helpful for your family.

College Plus also gives parents cd's now about helping kids find what direction they need to take and how to be good parents. For me, these cd's were good but not earth-shattering.

We enjoyed our coaching calls at first because we were so clueless, but after a while they seemed unnecessary.

And a biggie about College Plus: they don't seem to encourage kids to get started early on college anymore. To me they seem to be putting a lot of extra burdens on parents. Instead of avoiding the repetitive parts of college and high school, College Plus seems to be encouraging high school students to join their program, College Prep. Then they pressure parents about "making sure they are teaching all the right courses to their kids to prepare them for college." The parents I know already feel all of these pressures but actually need to be released from them in some ways. And some of the classes that College Prep insists are "necessary" are classes that my oldest child, the one who got his master's degree when he was 18, never had. In my opinion, he did fine anyway. And when Treehouse was looking for an employee to hire and bless, they certainly didn't care if he had had the classes either.

But if you want to do this new way, but you're really freaking out, and you have the money, you could do College Plus for one year. (or for the whole program.)

Did I Hear Something About Liberty?

Yes. You could also do Liberty University's dual credit program. Some say that you can get a degree for about $10,000, and if you're wanting to save your child's heart from the Frat House lifestyle, online Liberty may be the way to go. Students can take classes like Bible, Theology, Philosophy, Apologetics ... Imagine college drawing your child closer to the Lord instead of away from Him!

Liberty charges (at the moment) about $500 for a dual credit class, compared to $1200 for a regular class. Two classes per 8 week term. At Liberty you can get a dual credit degree in a year or two this way. You test out of all classes except about 10-15, depending on the degree.

Also consider degreesavvy.com. At the time of writing, only the beta version is up and running, but this is the actual website of Deep Throat! I mean

Julie the Genius! She has been such a help to us in guiding us about how to think outside the box.

But I am getting ahead of myself.

How Old Do You Have to Be to Take a CLEP Test?

A kid can take a CLEP test at any age I guess (official rules and testing center locations can be found at CollegeBoard.Org). Micah didn't actually enter a school until age 16 when he got his official acceptance to Thomas Edison State College in New Jersey. Kind of weird, I know! (It is normal to have to read the previous two sentences several times. I think I had to myself just now.) It will make more sense later.

Okay, but what about a GED?

None of my kids have taken the GED. I do not advise homeschooled students to take the GED. Why take it?

I was an admissions counselor for our little Christian college, and I knew the GED carries a stigma with it. When we had students apply to the college who already had at least 30 hours of college credits, they didn't have to give us any information about their high school work — just about their college work.

So please do not take the GED just because you are homeschooled. And don't take it just because you're skipping high school. If you are a homeschool mom or dad, YOU are the principal, and you get to decide what your high school curriculum is. In Oregon, where I live, homeschool IS a private school. *If your high-school-aged child is studying for college finals, your child is receiving a superior education. Hello! You have an amazing kid! A GED will only make your child look like a high school dropout.*

The Lady that I Talked to at the College Said Some Things that Contradicted What You Said

So let me guess. You called a college, and the employee said you have to be enrolled at their college to take a CLEP test. And you have to have a monkey on your shoulders. And there is no such thing as a CLEP test. And you have to give all the employees chocolates before you take it. Hmmmm ... Let me just say that many of the employees at colleges do not know what they are talking about when it comes to getting a degree through tests. This whole testing idea is a very well-kept secret.

Think about it! If everyone knew they could get their accredited degree for a fraction of the cost, all of the colleges would go out of business! If Christian parents knew their kids could still walk with the Lord after college and not turn into Feminist Communists, if students knew they could study in their pajamas and fuzzy slippers at their own pace, if older professionals knew they could get their degree in a year or two, if grandparents knew there was a way out of co-signing for loans which will never be paid, everyone would be doing this.

All this is to say that college employees may not have heard of what you're doing because not many are doing it yet. You are one of the few blessed people who have heard of this amazing approach to getting an accredited degree. So they may give you wrong information just because they are not very familiar with this whole new approach to college.

If an employee tells you something that doesn't sound right, call a bigger college and ask the same question. If their answer sounds more like what you read in this book, call the small college back and say for instance, "Um, the University of Texas Testing

Office said this. Does that sound right to you?"
Always be polite and kind in your interactions with
these people. They could become your friends as
they have for us. They will be amazed at what you
are doing.

There is also the possibility that, although I update
this book all the time, something has changed again,
as it does frequently in this morphing system.
Someday maybe everybody will be testing to get
their degrees. Until then, it is constantly changing.

It would also be a good idea to take the funny
information you heard from the college employee
and ask about it on one of the forums:

CLEP4Homeschool on Yahoo

or

Instacert.com

A Word from Micah about what it Feels Like When Your Mom Wants you to be Above Grade Level: Do You Like it, Micah?

Keep them above grade level!! It has been really motivating to us that Mom lets us do work above what our age would be doing. We got so excited about studying. It has been an exciting journey, and I was able to get my Bachelor of Arts in Social Sciences by age 16.

But My Son is 13, and He Hasn't Even Taken Any College Tests Yet

Oh, wow. Are you kidding?! This program is for people of any age, and you are getting a great start if you are starting now. We weren't as ambitious with our next few kids, and they will probably graduate when they are somewhere around 22, 18, and 17 respectively. And this whole thing works great for older adults who want to go back to school. Look at all the pictures of students on tesc.edu. They are all older than traditionally aged college students.

What if My Kids Aren't Able to Excel Like That?

Great question. One of the beautiful characteristics of home schooling is that your child's program can be tailor-made to suit him. He can learn to read earlier than a public school child, or if he needs to, he can learn to read later. I have some of both in my family. I even have a dyslexic child who is doing beautifully with CLEP tests. Sometimes these kind of learning methods are even better for the hyperactive kid who gets excited. Because being above grade-level is exciting!! They may have a rough start at first (like any student starting CLEP's), but they may sail through it later when they are in the groove of test-taking. God made each of us to be unique, not like robots.

I would encourage you to not stress about the less important subjects. My kids love history and know more than I ever will about it, but it is not because I have forced them to drill history facts. It is because they have no tv, no video games to play, and they have a lot of time to read the interesting history books that are laying around the house. I let them read historical fiction when they are done with their math every day. I buy them fascinating Dover coloring books (geared toward older elementary kids), and go with Gregg Harris's idea of "delight-directed study".

Even my dyslexic child has amazed me by being able to conquer subjects that I thought would be impossible, even at an age ahead of peers. Labels did not hinder this child. What labels? Often these children don't even realize when they are behind because in a homeschool setting they are not surrounded by peers. That is what happened in our house. And guess what. Now we have a dyslexic student doing college-level work during high school.

How Do I Study for the Tests?

One thing you can do is to get high school textbooks about the same subject. (Remember that college is often a repeat of high school?!)

Also there is a website that is really helpful to my kids that quizzes test takers on the material. You can actually use it (instacert.com or instantcert.com) to learn it when you know absolutely nothing. *Most students study a text book as well as Instacert for each test.*

Instacert is made of computerized "flash cards". Micah, Hannah, Josh, and Matt often went to the site knowing almost nothing about the subject and just went through the cards to learn what the questions were (This means their first scores for that subject

was like a zero. That's what you're supposed to do).
Then they went through them again and again, trying
for a better and better "score", until they were ready
to take their CLEP tests. When we use it, it is $30/
month.

Sometimes we accidentally kept paying for Instacert,
even though Micah wasn't using it that month. The
company was always very kind with us, giving us our
money back on our word that we hadn't needed it
the past couple of months that we paid! (Of course,
we ask that you don't take advantage of their
kindness). Nowadays we seem to always have
someone studying for a CLEP test, so we are regular
Instacert junkies. No need for us to call them and
say we're not using it this month! We are hooked.

What Do I Do When I am Ready to Take a Test?

Go to the CLEP website:

http://clep.collegeboard.org/

Pay for your CLEP test online. The website will walk
you through the whole process. Remember this is
the College Board, the same people who administer

the SAT. *You will pay online for the test and then pay another fee at the testing center/college.*

If you click on the CLEP website that you are a student and that you are ready to get started, the site will tell you 5 steps:

1. *Find out your institution's CLEP credit policy.* Remember that if Thomas Edison State College is your institution, and I recommend that it be just that, their policy is that they accept any CLEP test.
2. *Decide which exam(s) to take.* I recommend that Analyzing and Interpreting Literature be your first exam.
3. *Register to Take and Exam.* You can create an account on the website, and they will keep all your CLEP scores for 20 years! My kids have taken these tests at many testing centers, even overseas, and they were all credited to their own account without trouble. You don't have to take the test at the college that you want to graduate from. **Be sure to print your registration ticket to present to the test center on test day.**
4. *Schedule test day with your test center.* You can find a testing center on the CLEP site. Then call the testing department of that college and see what appointments they have open. If you realize you're not going to be ready for the test when your date gets closer, just cancel your appointment and reschedule when you feel more ready. But one thing my husband realized is that sometimes you need to go ahead and take the test so you won't

forget what you learned in the beginning of your study time!

5. *Prepare for your exam(s).* I recommend the Official CLEP Study Guide and the resources recommended on your forums, Instacert and CLEP4Homeschool Yahoo Group. And of course you should start preparing for your test before you make your appointment because otherwise you have no way of knowing when you will be ready to take the test.

What if I Fail a Test?

Then you are just like a Cooksey! Oh, we've failed lots of tests. When that happens, remind yourself how much this class would have cost if it was at a local university. Look at the cost per credit hour and then multiply it by 3 or 6! Also remember the time you saved. It probably didn't take as long as a college semester (for instance, January through May) to study for this test. You are doing awesome!

Now pick up your jaw off of the floor, and remind yourself that it's okay to fail a few tests. Especially if this is your first test, expect that you may fail it. I promise it's okay. It gets much easier when you are used to doing tests all the time.

If you fail a test (and you probably will. Nothing personal. Ha.) you have a few options:

1. Study again and take the same test after 6 months (there is a rule that you can't take it before then). One of my kids failed Western Civilization II twice! We moved on after that...
2. Take a similar test. For instance if you failed the English Composition CLEP (By the way, the one with the essay is easier!), try taking the English Composition I TECEP test.
3. You could also find another test that you feel more comfortable with that counts for the same credit. One of my kids failed the Biology test and was able to take the Computer Science test for his Science credit. The Computer Science test is pretty easy.

TECEP tests: (from www2.tesc.edu/listalltecep.php tells which courses these count for, and if you click on the test it will tell you a paragraph about the test)

English Composition:
English Composition I
English Composition II

Humanities:
Public Relations Thought and Practice
Technical Writing
Introduction to News Reporting

Social Sciences:

World History from 1600 to Present
Introduction to Political Science
Introduction to Comparative Politics
Psychology of Women (sounds weird)
Abnormal Psychology (I don't recommend this one)
Marriage and the Family (surely a liberal perspective)

Natural Sciences/Mathematics:
The Science of Nutrition
Applied Liberal Arts Mathematics
College Algebra
Principles of Statistics

Business and Management:
Principles of Financial Accounting
Principles of Managerial Accounting
Federal Income Taxation
Business in Society
Strategic Management
Computer Concepts and Applications
Security Analysis and Portfolio Management
Financial Institutions and Markets
Marketing Communications
Sales Management
Advertising
Negotiations and Conflict Management
Operations Management

Computer Science Technology:
Network Technology

Applied Science and Technology:

Medical Terminology
Radiation Safety Officer

What Do I Do When I'm Confused about Something?

Ask your question on the forums or see if someone else already asked your question:

Instacert.com (degreeforum.net)

or

CLEP4Homeschool on Yahoo

When I Get Stumped About Which Test to Take Next, What Do I Do?

Take a look at the internet forums about CLEP tests. Lots of folks are there ready to help you figure out your journey. Instacert.com has a forum that you can use, even if you aren't paying for their service at that time. They also have a forum that is only for current members, but you can learn a lot from the free forum.

Instacert.com or Instantcert.com
Yahoo group: Clep4Homeschool

The Instacert forum mainly has posts from students, and the Yahoo group mainly has posts from moms whose kids are working on degrees.

Many students wisely group their tests together. If you are studying about history that goes with another history test, take them right after another one! But don't be a perfectionist (I struggle with that.) You can't plan this journey perfectly.

One of my kids took Educational Psychology after Psychology. Things like that.

Some people take two tests in one day! Wow. That seems really hard to me. But do what works for you.

Do I Get a Degree Plan Like a Regular College?

Yes. More on that later.

Have I Heard of Anyone Else that Does College This Way?

The Duggar family from the show, 19 Kids and Counting, said in their book, *A Love that Multiplies* that

> "[S]everal of [our] older children [are] beginning the process of earning a college degree through College Plus! This program lets students earn a bachelor's degree in a fraction of the time and for much less money than enrolling in a traditional brick-and-mortar college."
>
> There is a very clear explanation of the outside-the-box college experience in pages 157 and 158 of their book.

Do You Get a Diploma, or Do You Have to Make a Fake One?

Ha ha! After Micah had 90 hours of college credits from tests, he applied to Thomas Edison State College in New Jersey. That is far from where we live in Oregon, but that's okay.

Since he was only 16, he had to also send a letter appealing that although he was young, he was a "highly motivated student". He (and we) are not sure that he is actually "highly motivated," but that is what they wanted us to say.

After changing the deadline for us several times, Thomas Edison accepted him as a student! Suddenly the telephone staff went from acting offended that we had bothered their coffee break to delighted to help us!

After he passed all the required courses (tests), he applied for graduation (just like at a regular college). Maybe that was the one they kept moving the deadline for us. Anyway, one day we got the word that YES! He could graduate! Woohoo!! The grand experiment worked! I could stop having figurative heart attacks!!

We were invited to attend the graduation ceremony, and although Micah's grandma offered to pay his way to New Jersey, Micah opted to stay home and have a quiet party with his church friends. We received a GORGEOUS DIPLOMA *representing **his accredited degree**,* and he started graduate school.

Update: Indoctrination Class

Although TESC offers online classes, Micah did not have to take any classes at all because his Social Sciences major allowed him to test out of every single one. Now there is a required class for all students. I have heard that it has something to do with requirements from the Common Core Curriculum.

This class teaches "tolerance." Socialism, feminism, the homosexual agenda, and other philosophies are to be embraced, et cetera. It is called **Liberal Arts Capstone**. So far we have not found any colleges that offer a similar class from a more evangelical/ conservative perspective that could be transferred to TESC. Many times, "capstone" means that it cannot be transferred in. At the time of this update, tuition per credit at TESC is $250, so if Liberal Arts Capstone is a 3-hour class, it costs $750.

So Christian parents would make a good choice to opt for online Liberty University in Virginia over Thomas Edison State College. But this would require at least 10 - 15 classes taken online, which would up the cost of your child's degree.

If parents have the money and time for Liberty, I say, "Go for it!" But I wouldn't encourage anyone to go into debt for Liberty over one class that they were worried about.

When Micah was studying for his Fine Arts CLEP test, there were paintings that he was supposed to be familiar with that we didn't think were appropriate. How did we know this? Because his computer was in the living room, in full view of everyone walking by. I don't recommend handing your pubescent son a laptop with all internet sites available and saying, "Good-bye, son. I'm going to the grocery store!" We love and trust all of our kids, but we also know that we are all sinners:

"For all have sinned and fall short of the glory of God." (Romans 3:23)

And we also know that we are to:

"put on the Lord Jesus Christ, and make no provision for the flesh, to fulfill its lusts." (Romans 13:14)

I believe that giving a young man that much temptation is making provision for his flesh. After he has obtained victory in his life, then he can have more privileges, but he still needs accountability, either from his parents, his wife, a pastor, or a friend.

Soooo ....
All this to say that Micah didn't study the parts of Instacert that we felt were ungodly, and we told him that if he didn't pass the test, that would be okay. We would be very proud of him. But guess what! He passed anyway!

We also ran into some problems with the American Literature test and Geriatrics. We switched him to English Literature instead of American, and that worked well.

He learned ridiculous things for Geriatrics, but he knew it was silly. We thought he had to have the test. It turned out that he didn't even need it after all! But my point is that he survived the ungodly propaganda.

The beauty of it was that we were here to walk through it with him! If he had been in another state in a dorm room by himself, we wouldn't have been there to support him, be his best friends, and help him think through what he was hearing.

I am hoping that the Liberal Arts Capstone class is something that my kids will be able to survive, we will have good discussions, and they will come out stronger than they were before. This has happened in other areas. The main thing is, BE THERE for your kids to have these discussions with. As S.M. Davis pointed out, Jesus was always asking his disciples questions. Ask your kids:

What is God teaching you lately?

Is God answering your prayers?

Is there anything questionable that you're having to study?

Have you been having fun lately?

What is your favorite thing you did last week?

Do you have any questions about what we believe?

What have you been reading in your Bible lately?

Tell your kids that you are ALWAYS available to answer their questions. Tell them they are always welcome to ask you if there is something they feel is inconsistent in your life.

There isn't a certain answer that is "correct" with some of these questions. You just want to spark discussion. Build the relationship. Be willing to spend time with them. Talk. Heart to heart. And you know what? LISTEN.

But as a Homeschool Mom I so Enjoy Stressing Over Trying to Make my Homeschool Like a Public School. I Love Making Transcripts! What Should I Do?

The above question is fake. No homeschool moms like making transcripts, and why should we make our home education just like the public school? If we wanted to do that, we could just ship our kids there like everyone else does.

Using the CLEP system with our oldest child, we never had to make a high school transcript.

Remember that by the time your child applies for admission at Thomas Edison, he may have over 90 hours of college credit. 30 hours plus makes him a transfer student, and colleges don't care about high school work once someone has 30 hours of college. So we never made a high school transcript with our oldest. That cuts down on homeschool mom mental health bills!

You know what's easier than making that perfect transcript? Checking "yes" on the Thomas Edison application where it says, "Did you graduate from high school?" Since my husband is the principal, and since Micah had already learned so much college-level material by then, Ronny declared him a graduate.

Update: My daughter Hannah would love to be a missionary. While this decision will depend on who she marries, she may try to be ready, with requirements met, before she gets married. The International Mission Board of the Southern Baptist Convention requires 12 hours of Bible credits for missionary wives.

So her senior year of high school, Hannah applied for scholarships. She might get her Bible credits at the College at Southwestern Baptist Theological Seminary, the College at Midwestern Baptist Theological Seminary. Why? Because Southern Baptist seminaries are very reasonably priced for Southern Baptist church members AND they have good doctrine!

When she applied for scholarships, some of them required a high school transcript. How long did it take us to make it? Less than a day. We found templates online, gave her credits for all her cooking, cleaning, and helping with younger siblings (Home Economics), dual credits for all her college tests, credits for all her math and other subjects, good grades because she had certainly earned them, and tried to not stress about it. I survived it. Woohoo!

So Do Your Kids Ace Every Subject?

No. None of us has ever been very good in Science for instance. Micah took Computer Science tests to qualify for those subjects.

Before CLEPping, Was Micah the Kind of Student Who Begged to Do Math Workbooks and Diagram Sentences?

No way. Most of the time when he was supposed to do his schoolwork, he stared at the end of his pencil!

But when we allowed him to take college-level tests he got excited! How fun to be able to say he was ahead of schedule! He got motivated and sometimes even studied on weekends and at night.

But My Children are not Self-motivated Like That. They Think Schoolwork is Boring.

Micah would be the first to tell you that he is just like the rest of us – He has trouble with self-motivation, too.

My husband Ronny is great during our kids' testing because he helps them set goals, and he goes ahead and schedules their tests to get them motivated to study. Right now the rule is that Josh and Matt can make a CookseyCubMedia.com video whenever they have taken a new test.

Usually Ronny would take Micah to his tests and work on sermons, etc, (he is a pastor) in the car while he waited on Micah to finish.

Ronny's philosophy was that if Micah had been studying for a while on a subject, he would go ahead and schedule the test so that he didn't forget what he had studied in the beginning.

Come on, tests!! All the more funny videos for us to watch!

But I Don't Want My Resume to Say That I Graduated from "Mickey Mouse Mail-Order Institute."

Oh no, no! Of course it won't! Ha! I have a relative who has done a fellowship at Harvard and is now a partner in a law firm a couple of states away from New Jersey, where Thomas Edison State College is. I mentioned the college to her, thinking, "this is a good test." I knew that she is sometimes a part of hiring people and would know of nearby universities.

When I said he was going to TESC, she said, "Oh, I've heard of that!"

Believe me, I come from a long line of opinionated folks, and she is very concerned about the education of her releatives. If she thought it was a lesser institution, she would have told me!

I Took a CLEP Test, and the First Thing that Happened was a Ridiculously Long Tutorial on How to Use a Computer! I Thought Maybe There was Something Weird Going On.

Actually, that happens at the beginning of every test. It is possible to fast forward though it, but I recommend suffering through it at least your first test to make sure you know all of it. Be prepared for how ridiculous it is!

I'm a Christian Mom, and I Don't Feel Comfortable with My Kids Being on the Internet to Study. There is So Much Bad Media on the Internet.

I totally agree. That is why we put **Safe Eyes**, a parental control software, on our teens' computers. In fact, we use Safe Eyes to blacklist ALL sites except the ones we approve! Then we MANUALLY whitelist the sites we want our kids on.

UPDATE: We had to stop using Safe Eyes because our kids' computers were too old! We get used old Macintoshes on Craig's List for cheap, and they work well for us. But when we couldn't use Safe Eyes anymore, that presented a problem. Instead, we now just use **Parental Controls** on the Macintoshes. Just like when we had Safe Eyes, we BLACKLIST EVERYTHING. Then manually whitelist the sites like Instacert.com and TESC.edu. Parental controls can also be used for Kindles.

You might also want to utilize **Covenant Eyes**, which sends parents a report of what sites a computer has visited. We do.

We also use **www.clea.nr** for erasing the crazy stuff that violates all of us after we watch clean videos. With clea.nr, you don't have to see ANY suggestions for what the Youtube folks want you to see. It is a "cleaner" for your internet.

Another very simple safeguard: **password protection** for your phones, ipads, computers, and smart tv's that don't have most everything blacklisted. This allows Mom, Dad, and older kids who have victory in their lives (and may need a lot of internet access for work, etc.) to not have to wrangle with internet filters every time they're trying to look up a recipe or something important. You should still have Covenant Eyes for every computer so everyone has accountability.

When our teenage boys need to look up something on a blacklisted site (which is almost every site in the world!), we type the password for them and ask them to sit next to a sibling who can see what they're doing.

K9 is another option a lot of people like. It is free, but it doesn't really work for us.

And don't forget about putting your computers in public places, facing out for all to see what is being viewed. Glass doors for home offices can also come in handy. (Thank you, titus2.org for that idea!)

Whatever you use, use something. Your children's hearts are at risk.

Do Your Kids Work on Several Tests at Once or One at a Time?

One at a time. But sometimes they take related tests in succession, such as Educational Psychology right after Psychology.

Most CLEPs are related to history, so many of them are grouped beautifully together. For instance "Civil War and Reconstruction" could be taken soon after someone had studied for "American History, 1865 to the Present."

At the time of this update, my sons Josh and Matt just finished several history tests that related to each other because they were about history in the 1900's:

The Cold War
Russian History
The Vietnam War

Modern Middle East
Civil War and Reconstruction
American History, 1865 - Present
Western Europe
Europe from 1945 - Present

Do We Need to Enroll Right Away?

My wonderful friend Julie (Deep Throat) who has researched all this has informed me that the rules have changed! These new rules are going to make things much easier for you and even save you stress and money. Woohoo!!

In the past, students had to pay $1700 - $3000 as an enrollment fee, even if they took no classes at the Thomas Edison State College. In the past, we had to not enroll at the college until we have over 100 hours of testing credit. The reason was that once you enrolled in Thomas Edison State College, you had to start paying the large enrollment fee, even if you were only taking CLEP tests and no TESC classes.

As for Liberty University, you would want to check with them on this. My understanding is that they are more of a traditional college that doesn't charge a large enrollment fee, only tuition and other fees (which would be much smaller than TESC's enrollment fee).

Okay. Now TESC is like all the other colleges. You just pay for the classes that you take. Hooray! There are several kinds of tests you can take, such as CLEP, Excelsior, and DANTES. There are also TECEP's.

TECEP's are Thomas Edison tests. These cost about the same amount as a CLEP test. Maybe less because for TECEP's you don't have to pay the college an additional fee.

Thomas Edison now requires students to take a minimum number of hours at their own college. They include Thomas Edison classes as well as Thomas Edison tests (TECEP's). They require:

for an Associate's degree: 12 hours of TESC classes or tests
for a Bachelor's degree: 24 hours of TESC classes or tests

Again, this is much better than the old system.

May I Just Ask, Why Do You Like Your Kids to Be Above Grade Level?

- This takes pressure off of the already pressured homeschool mom. If her kids are above grade level, she doesn't have to stress about boosting her kids up all the time, finishing the book before the end of the year, etc.
- So much of the work we all did in public schools was time-wasting busy work. I was a public school teacher and watched kids waste hours and hours of time. Each student had to find something to do while the slower kids finished their work.
- As Christians, we must value every minute! Why do pages of addition problems if the child already understands the concepts? Skipping ahead gives more time for Kingdom work. **(Please remember that skipping ahead is completely different than pressuring kids to get tons of schoolwork done in order to move ahead. Our kids only school in the morning! We require them to learn all the math concepts and are flexible with the other subjects. Don't pressure your kids to grow up too fast!)**
- If they need extra time on a subject, no problem because they started ahead of schedule in the beginning of it.
- Finishing college early means that they hopefully will not be trying to do college while

they are married. In many cases, this saves them from financial heartaches.
- Finishing college early means that our sons could even get master's/seminary degrees before marriage. (Micah did. The MATS degree is very short, and at a Southern Baptist seminary it is very reasonably priced for SBC church members)
- College is often just a repeat of high school anyway, so why worry so much about high school? Do you really feel like your high school subject matter benefited you that much?
- Recording all of my kids' high school credits is much harder than what I am doing with my older students. They basically study on their own! No crazy recording systems to make a transcript.
- If the government asks to validate what a homeschool family is doing, they will be impressed that the children are above grade level. Educators (again, I was a public school teacher) do not generally worry about the grades or materials that were skipped if the children are able to complete high-level assignments already.
- The kids get excited about school if they know they are above where they should be in their work!
- Excited students retain more information than bored students.
- Skipping ahead saves time.
- Testing out of college classes saves time.

- College at home saves TONS of money.
- College at home means my children are not living in an ungodly atmosphere without accountability.
- College at home means that my children are not sitting under ungodly professors.
- An alarming number of Christian students are lost to secularism after age 18. Something like 85%. If I sent my children away, I would be gambling with all the precious years I have poured into their lives.

At the time of this update, I have a nine-year-old child who is very bright. (I guess that would be about third grade) But he is very hard to motivate, especially with boring tasks.

He really needed help with his basic math facts at the beginning of the year. But I knew that if we worked on math facts, that's all we would get done all year in math because he would drag his feet so much. I knew he would catch on to more advanced math principles if I gave him a chance.

So we worked on multiplication facts for a while and then scrapped that. We put it on the back burner for later.

Then we dove into fractions and other fifth grade math subjects. It was great! If he needed to know a math fact that he hadn't worked hard enough on, I pointed out how important it was and made him figure it out. But he really thrived on those advanced concepts, and we learned so much this year!

Now it is June 4, and I have told him that he needs to keep doing a math page every day, even though it is summer vacation. When he really masters multiplication facts, addition and subtraction up to 18, carrying, and borrowing, then he can stop school for the year. Until then, he does math in the summer.

This is obviously motivating him to get going and learn those facts! I know this is unconventional. Remember my degree is in elementary education of math! Why would I do 5th grade math with a 3rd grader, then go back to 2nd grade concepts? Well, all I can say is that it is working, and I am grateful for the medium of homeschooling. It allows for flexibility, motivation, advanced concepts, and a tailor-made program for each student.

As Mike Farris has so wisely pointed out, school-at-home has always been the education method of kings. It allows for private tutoring and one-on-one instruction. Great student-teacher ratio.

I Heard Something About FEMA Credits.

Yes, in the past students could get 30 hours of free online credit in about two weeks from the Federal Emergency Management Association. This was great! But unfortunately, Thomas Edison does not accept those credits anymore. There is one college that does accept them, and it gives an Associates degree in Emergency Management. I'm not sure what that college is. But do not fret. The new rules at Thomas Edison State College make life (and even finances) easier for you!

Chapter 2: What is My VERY VERY First Step? *Some more how to's.*

Step 1: The very first thing you want to do is to pray to our **Father, which art in Heaven.**

He created the entire world in 6 days, so He has all the power to help you through this maze. He is exponentially the most powerful being in the Universe. In fact, He created the very Universe of which we speak and in which we live!

The scientific evidence of the origins of matter point to Biblical Creationism. But because of spiritual darkness, people's eyes are blinded, and people choose to believe in ridiculously unlikely stories such as the Big Bang and Evolution. They are so unlikely, in fact, that scientists have said, "Well, we know this is unlikely. That is why it must have taken billions of years." Scientists know this because they have studied statistics and probability.

The whole idea of the Big Bang or of Evolution violates the Second Law of Thermodynamics, that the Universe always moves from order to disorder, not the other way around.

All fossils are of fully-formed creatures. There is not a single fossil of a half-and-half animal. There are too many missing links, and there is too much to deny an intelligent Designer or Creator.

Whale bones have been found in the Andes Mountains, indicating a worldwide flood. In fact, every major religion in the world records a worldwide flood.

Chariot wheels were found in the bottom of the Red Sea, validating the Biblical account of the Children of Israel escaping Pharaoh.

Sea fossils cover the Grand Canyon, again pointing to a worldwide flood. The fossils appear to have been petrified all at once in a catastrophic event.

Don't be fooled by "scientific studies" that try to exalt themselves above God Himself, the Creator of every scientist. Even the study in the 1950's that "proved" that saturated fats cause heart attacks has now been shown to be bogus and skewed. In fact, it has caused more people to eat starches and sugars, which has caused more heart attacks than before its great "enlightenment." God is always smarter than scientists.

Give this whole idea of a cheaper, faster way of doing college to the God of the Universe, and ask Him if it is right for you and your family. Thank Him for this great opportunity.

Ask Him for the strength and wisdom to get it done. Commit your whole life to Him. Repent of all sin, ask Him to forgive you for every wrong you have done, and purpose to live the rest of your life for Him. Ask him that this degree would be used for His glory, and not for your own.

Ask Him to guide you through the whole process. Ask Him to help you become closer to Him through it. Ask God to take you to Heaven when you die, and ask Him to use you to glorify His Son Jesus while you are still on this earth.

Step 2: Pick a Major and College

TESC accepts the most test credits, so most choose TESC. If you are dead set on graduating from a college that is not featured on the College Plus homepage, you need to **check that college's website to see which CLEP tests they accept and what scores they require**. Very important.

Although Thomas Edison State College does try to hide their catalog from you, *and their catalog changes from time to time,* and the staff at TESC usually seem offended when you call to ask questions:

e.g. "What's ya' problem already? I was trying to eat my sandwich for cryin' outloud."

you *can* download their catalog from their webpage if you are persistent enough. Remember to rely on your friends at the Instacert forums. They will tell you what worked for them.

You can enroll in the college so they will be nicer to you on the phone, but remember that costs more than $1000/year.

College Plus also lists the possible majors at:

collegeplus.org/majors

You can also go to CollegePlus.org and click on "majors."

Factors to consider when choosing a major:

1. **Some majors allow for more elective credit than others do.** There are a lot of CLEP and DANTES tests that could count as electives. So, if your major calls for less electives, your degree will be more expensive and more time-consuming. (You can see what is required for each major in the TESC catalog. Keep in mind that the catalog changes. If it changes significantly, your friends at the Instacert forums will probably mention it.
2. **Some majors require TESC (Thomas Edison State College) classes or Liberty University classes.** Again, this makes your degree more expensive and time-consuming.
3. **Some majors, like nursing, would require you to take classes at a local college.** Again

more time and money. This is what the older Duggar girls are studying.

4. **If you are a parent of a very young college student, remember that any class could mean ungodly content under the supervision of someone you don't know.** Since Micah, Josh, and Matt were so young, we chose to do the quickest, cheapest option: all testing and no classes. *They did still have ungodly content in some of their tests, but we were here to guide them through it. We were also not worried about our boys getting practical degrees because they all wanted seminary degrees when they graduated. We figured that even for a secular job, having a master's degree on their resume would make them employable, especially if they got their degrees when they were young. That has proven true for our oldest son, and the other two are still testing.*

5. **One disadvantage to choosing a degree plan that does not require any classes is that you will not have a GPA!** (grade point average) This has not been a problem for Micah. When he applied for his Master of Arts in Theological Studies at Midwestern Baptist Theological Seminary (a short online degree that is very economical for Southern Baptist church members), the Admissions Staff thought it unusual that he had no GPA and was so young, but they accepted him at first on a provisional basis. After he performed well the

first semester, he was fully accepted. They even did a feature article about Micah in their seminary magazine! (Update: Now that TESC requires an indoctrination class for every degree, this may not be an issue anymore. In other words, there may not be any more degrees anywhere that are accomplished solely through tests.)

More on Ungodly Content

As I mentioned, do watch out for some of the paintings in the study material (including Instacert) for the Fine Arts test. Also, American Literature has some ridiculous "classics" to study that I would say have very low merit. We chose the British Literature test instead.

The Gerontology Excelsior Test included some foolishness about ending the lives of precious older people early.

My husband told Micah that he didn't have to study those parts, and if he failed the tests, we would not worry about it at all! As I mentioned, he passed the tests anyway. Thank You, God!!

Step 3: Now You Need a Degree Plan

A degree plan tells you exactly what tests you need to take and for which courses they will count. Micah started out as an English major. Then we decided to go with History so he could finish faster. Then the catalog changed, and we changed again to Social Sciences to allow for a lot of elective credits. You have several options here:

1. Sign up for **College Plus** for only one year, especially if you are over age 18. If you are over age 18, College Plus will not make you defer to "College Prep," which is, in my estimation, very different than going ahead and starting your degree full force. You can get 12 college credits during high school through their dual credit program, but in my estimation, you could do so much more. 12 credits is only 1/2 of a year of college. Anyway, College Plus will give you your **degree plan during this time as well as coaching calls for a year**. Since college through testing can be a complicated maze, College Plus is nice to have around to guide you. Their staff is very kind and accommodating. At the time of writing, each year with College Plus costs around **$6500**.

Most exams cost a little more than $100 (plus your fee to the testing center) whether or not you pay for College Plus, and your text for each test may cost around $20.

2. **You really can figure this out yourself.** Yes, it is confusing. But if you download the TESC catalog, give this thing to God constantly and ask for His help, you *can* figure it out. Sign up for Instacert.com, read the archived forums, and outline what degree you want. Don't forget about the Yahoo group, Clep4Homeschool, too.

Thomas Edison State College Catalog Link:
http://www.tesc.edu/academics/ academicprograms.php

There is a little brown box in the middle of the page that says, "Access Our Online College Catalog." Download it by clicking the button, remember that the catalog is updated from time to time, so keep checking it.

You said Your Son's Degree was $8000, but My Son's was $8005.

I'm so sorry about that! Micah's was probably closer to $7K, but we wanted to guess high and be sure we were not underestimating. I'm sure the cost of CLEP tests, fees, books, and even lollipops will continue to increase. But I'm hoping that our story can help many students to save bundles instead of going the traditional route.

Where Does Micah Work Now?

Well, when he was little he made bird houses and sold his old toys door-to-door. Not what you wanted to know? Then he mowed lawns, then made web pages for people, then worked at a Christian university (Isn't that ironic?!), and now he works for a company called Treehouse.

I like Treehouse because it is also an educational tool that thinks outside the box. I think it is great for homeschoolers because it allows students of any age to learn computer skills online. A homeschooler could do Treehouse lessons as part of his curriculum in junior high or high school and soon be writing apps and websites! He could use this money to help pay for college (as Micah did for his Master's degree) **or just forgo college all together because he has marketable skills**. Treehouse even offers online classes on marketing and how to start a business.

My daughter Bethany learned some programming on Treehouse when she was only 12 years old. If Micah were here, he would point out that Treehouse is an app with entertaining incentives, not just a site with videos.

Step 4: Take a CLEP Test

Where do you begin? If you have familiarized yourself with the King James Bible or other Old English literature, you might consider taking Analyzing and Interpreting Literature.

This is the exam that Micah took in Tokyo when he was 12, sitting next to the 50-year-old man.

We didn't know Micah should brush up on or practice answering English comprehension questions, so he made a 51 – he passed by one point!

Take a look at the Instacert forums or CLEP4Homeschool on Yahoo before you take the test, and find out what helped others and what they suggest studying.

Should I Fly to Tokyo to Take that Test?

Oh, no, of course not! We just happened to be living there at the time because we were missionaries with the International Mission Board of the Southern Baptist Convention for ten years. (What a great organization and a great opportunity for all of us!)

If you do happen to live overseas, you can check the CLEP website for testing sites. At that time, Asia only afforded Temple University in Tokyo and somewhere in Kuala Lampur, Malaysia.

Actually, no matter where you live, check the site for a great testing center that you prefer. You might try several and see where you feel most comfortable. Or if you like the first one you try (as much as a person can "like" a testing center!), stick with it. That way you won't be distracted by changing surroundings.

Micah enjoyed going back to the same small setting where the proctors knew him (and forgave him when he washed his i.d. in his jean pocket).

What if I Totally Don't Get Old English?

That is completely fine! This is your first test! You have many, many to choose from. Choose one that sounds interesting.

You may notice some tests on your degree plan do not say "CLEP." You could save those for the end. These may require a different testing center, a little more money, and a little different mind-frame. Some people stick with CLEPs at first – College Level Exam Program.

Josh and Matt did take some DANTES tests in the beginning because they were studying so much history that it made sense to group the DANTES histories with the CLEP histories. Do what works for you.

The most motivating CLEPs to start with are the ones that gift you 6 hours of credit for just one exam! I recommend choosing one of those first.

How Do I Study for the Tests?

Sign up for Instacert.com (also goes by InstantCert.com). Learn the flashcards. Read up on the test on the forums.

Some of Micah's exams he only used Instacert, and he still passed. That may not be you. That is fine. Especially since this is your first test, I recommend buying a high school-level textbook and brushing up. If you are a Christian, you can buy Bob Jones or Abeka textbooks. You can also buy **Peterson's Guides for specific tests.**

Instacert may not offer study cards for every exam. If that is the case, go to the library or bookstore, and read up on your subject. But even if Instacert doesn't have flashcards for your test, the forums probably have helpful info about the test.

When you feel ready for the CLEP, **take a practice test from the CLEP Official Study Guide by the College Board.** *Peterson's Guides are helpful, but remember that the College Board book is official!*

Did you pass the practice test? Then you may be ready!

I've Studied Enough for it. Now What?

You choose your testing center online at clep.collegeboard.org/started.

Now call them and set up a time to take the test.

College Board? Isn't That the Same People that Do the SAT?

You got it! The SAT people make CLEP tests.

Step 6: You Took Your Test. Now You Evaluate.

- Did you like your testing center? If not, try another one next time.
- Did you pass this one? It's so okay if you didn't! This is a new experience for you! Maybe you should re-evaluate your study methods. Ask for help on the forum.
  How long did it take you to get ready for the test? If you'd like to get your degree fast, maybe you should speed up. *Older students are often easily able to complete a CLEP degree in less than four years. Sometimes it only takes them a year!*

Step 7: Keep Studying, Keep Taking Tests, and Revel in the Excitement of All This Credit You are Amassing!

If you fail a test, either take it again in 6 months or find another one that would work better for the credit you need. You have to wait 6 months to take the same CLEP test again.

What if I Want to Take a Break? Will I Loose All My Hard Work and Have to Start Over Later?

CLEP scores are good for 20 years! You are sittin' pretty.

Step 8: Stay With it When Times Get Tough.

- If you are discouraged, get a friend to do it with you. You can encourage each other.
- Get encouragement from the Instacert forums or the Yahoo group (CLEP4Homeschool).
- Don't talk about it with people who don't get it. Most won't!
- Set goals for yourself.
- If coaching would be an encouragement to you, and if you have enough money, sign up for College Plus (collegeplus.org)
- Group similar tests one after the other to save work.
- Put encouraging Bible verses on your bathroom mirror.
- Tell yourself, "Only a short time left!"

- **Give it to God again! Ask for His strength and power.**

Step 9 or 10: When You are Sure You are Choosing Thomas Edison State College, Enroll in TESC. Or Liberty. Or wherever.

Please do not be intimidated by the application process. If you have taken college classes before, and your grade point average was a 2.0 or above, TESC will probably accept you! If your GPA is lower than that, they will probably accept you on probation. If you have no college credits except for tests, don't apply to TESC until you have at least 30 hours of credit. Then you won't have to make a high school transcript. Be prepared for an application fee of about $100.

Remember that if you are very young and you are applying to TESC, you need to check "yes" that you graduated from high school (look at the great education you got during your teen years!! Exponentially better than most.) *You will also need to include a letter saying that you are a "highly motivated student". (even if you're not! Ha!)*

Also remember that your testing credits will be transferred to the college, just as if you had taken classes somewhere else. (And if you do have college credits from other institution(s), request transcripts from those institutions to be sent to TESC as well. You will need to pay each of your past colleges a fee for the transcript.

Do not be discouraged if something doesn't count like you thought it would. Micah's expensive Excelsior exam actually ended up being worthless! You are still saving beaucoups of money compared to the indebted hamburger-flipping college graduates across the country! (And remember that if you can write on your resume that you finished your degree at an age younger than 22, that looks GREAT to an employer. If you are an older student who was able to finish college in less than four years, write that on your resume. Employers love that!)

You might want to wait until you have only TECEP tests left to enroll at TESC. (TECEP's are Thomas Edison tests). Why? Because since this field is so fluid, maybe something will change in the future, and TESC won't be the very best college for you to graduate from. Or maybe you will decide that you prefer a Christian education, and you want to go to Liberty. In that case, your TECEP's wouldn't transfer to any other college. So save your TECEP's and your enrollment to the end.

If you are applying to a college other than TESC, just ask the Admissions office what you need to do. They will spell it all out for you. Admissions offices like to answer questions about enrolling because that means more money for the college. Just ask that your other colleges send transcripts, transfer your test scores to your college, and take the classes you need to take to graduate.

One advantage to enrolling at TESC earlier would be that the employees would probably be more helpful with your questions! So if you prefer to enroll early, that is also an option. Chat with your forum buddies, and see what they recommend.

Step 9 or 10: When You're Through With CLEPs, Take the Other Tests on Your Degree Plan: Excelsior, DANTES, Thomas Edison Tests, and Others. Take the Classes You Need to Take (Micah didn't need any classes.)

When Micah took an **Excelsior exam**, he had to go to a very official testing center. It had a completely different atmosphere than the sweet Christian college he had been using. It was an office building in Portland, Oregon with very strict i.d. rules, etc. Just be prepared for that.

Also remember that some of these other tests are more expensive than CLEPs. Maybe $200-$300 each. TECEP's tend to be the same price as CLEP's.

Step 11: Since You are an Enrolled Student at TESC Now, the Staff Will Hopefully Answer Your Questions! Ask Them When They Recommend That You Apply for Graduation. Then Apply.

Again, do not worry about being accepted for graduation. If you pass what you need to pass, you can graduate! There will be a graduation fee that is probably over $300.

Step 12: Once All Your Requirements are Completed, Either Fly to New Jersey for Your Ceremony or Wait for Your Diploma at Home.

Congratulations! You worked hard for this!! Everybody is so proud of you. Take a great big breath, have a refreshing stretch, and roll your shoulders back.

You did it.

Appendix 1

Micah Cooksey

Micah Cooksey is one of the youngest graduate students to ever take classes at Midwestern. He's currently enrolled in the 100-percent online degree program offered through Midwestern Baptist College, SBC. He grew up on the mission field with his family, graduated from high school and college and is now pursuing his master's degree – all before the age of 18.

Here's a bit more about the spotlight student:

MW: *I understand that you grew up in a missionary family in Japan. Briefly tell us about the experience of growing up in that environment.*

MC: My family moved to Japan when I was 3-years old. When I was 13, we moved to McMinnville, Ore., which is where we live now. My dad is the pastor of Valley Baptist Church here. During the time my family spent in Japan, I learned to speak Japanese fluently, and I also gained an appreciation and an understanding for cultures that are different than ours.

MW: *You're 17-years old and taking seminary graduate classes. Tell us about your earlier schooling: Where did you attain your undergraduate degree? What was it in, and how old were you when you started those classes?*

MC: I was homeschooled through high school, and in June of 2010, I received my B.A. in Social Sciences from Thomas Edison State College, a distance learning institution. I was 12 when I started working on that degree (when I was still in Japan).

MW: *How did you hear about Midwestern's Master of Arts in Theological Studies degree program, and what interested you the most about pursuing this program track?*

MC: I heard about the degree through the Northwest Baptist Paper. The top thing for me about the MATS program is that I can take classes from home. My family and I had been praying about what the next step for my schooling should be, and the MATS program was perfect. If I go into missions with the International Mission Board, this would fulfill the degree requirements, which is another reason for my enrollment with this program.

MW: *What do you like best about the online format, and what's the most challenging aspect?*

MC: The thing I like most about the online format is its flexibility schedule-wise. Although there are deadlines at the end of each week, most of the coursework can be completed any hour of the day, unlike traditional classes. The most challenging aspect is the workload, especially since I'm taking two classes per seven-week term.

MW: *What has been your favorite class thus far, and why?*

MC: I would have to say that my favorite class to date was my hermeneutics course taught by Dr. David Sundeen. I really benefitted from taking that. In a way, though, every class has been my favorite because they are all so great.

MW: *At the pace you're moving, taking two classes per term, you're on track to finish your MATS degree by late 2011 or early 2012. What are your goals upon graduation?*

MC: I'm praying about doing one of two things: 1) going into ministry, possibly missions; or 2) studying either web design or marketing and getting a job in either of those fields.

MW: *Are any of your siblings on a course similar to what you've done?*

MC: Not exactly, but my sister, who is 14, is enrolled in a Christian paralegal program. We're still praying about whether or not my other siblings will follow a similar program to the one I'm doing. They'll definitely do something like it, but we're still praying about the exact details. **MW**

College From Home

Seminar

#1 - Anyone can do it!

- You don't have to be a child prodigy to do college from home

- You study a lot of what you would study in high school and get college credit

- On CLEP tests (offered by the Collegeboard, the writers of the SAT), you only have to get about half of the questions right to pass

#2 - It's faster and cheaper

- The average college student spends up to $100,000 or more and takes five years to finish

- With college from home, you can finish for about 1/10 of the cost of traditional college

- You can probably finish in one year if you go full time and you are at least 18 years old

#3 How do I do it?

Steps to earn your degree

(to be explained in detail later)

1. **Choose your major** (it's fine to change later - even

   multiple times)

2. **Take the tests**

3. **Enroll**

4. **Transfer your credits**

5. **Graduate**

Step 1: Choose Major

• Go to Thomas Edison's Website, TESC.edu. Don't be intimidated by the fact that it says, "Exclusively for Adults." They are trying to help older students realize that the staff is accustomed to working with students who are outside of the traditional 18-22 year age range.

• Click on *Academics,* then *What You Can Study*

• Look through the list of majors and choose the most appealing one. If it says, "Applied" in the major, that means that you can get college credit for work experience. This is great for older students who have been in the work force for a while. If this is you, then you would probably prepare a portfolio of work you have done that could earn you college credit. TESC could help you with that. A lot of other colleges also offer applied degrees for older students and are more than happy to explain how to do that. If you are a younger student, the majors list on the College Plus homepage might be less confusing to you.

- I changed from English to Humanities to Social Sciences, so don't stress this too much

- Remember: required courses mean more time and money. BUT they also may mean a more practical degree if you are not planning on going to graduate school. Practical degrees include business, nursing, and accounting.

Step 2: Take Tests

- On TESC's website, look at the credit distribution for your degree. This means there is a list that tells you exactly which course a test counts for.

- Using the TESC catalog, plug in tests to the appropriate subject areas

- Study for the test

- My favorite resource is Instacert.com

- Flaschcard-based study materials for most of the tests

- Instacert subscribers have access tot he exam-specific feedback area of degreeforum.net, which is very helpful

•A college or high school textbook is also good, particularly when used with Instacert. If you prefer a Christian perspective to your studies, you can study Christian textbooks, even though the tests themselves are not from a Christian perspective.

Step 3: Enroll

•After you are over 3/4 of the way through, enroll in TESC and begin taking the TECEP tests they require from you.

• Don't forget that you need to take the Liberal Arts Capstone class from TESC. Our sources say that this class may be mostly made up of writing assignments.

Step 4: Transfer Credits

- Transfer your transcripts to TESC's registrar. This means that you request that any college you have attended to send transcripts to TESC. Each of these colleges will charge you a fee for this service.

- Wait for TESC to evaluate your credits

- Be patient and don't panic if they put things in the wrong place - they usually switch things around before it is finished

- If you have questions, you can schedule a consultation with an academic advisor

- Finish taking the remaining tests and take any classes necessary

Step 5: Graduate

- Once everything is in order, you can go ahead and apply for graduation

- It's good to pick one of the four graduation dates and try to finish everything by the deadline for that date

- Remember, everything at TESC takes forever, so leave plenty of extra time

- If something happens and you are late, they occaisionally will make exceptions

Must Have's

•The "Official CLEP Study Guide" from the Collegeboard

•Cracking the Clep - a little outdated, but the general

principles still apply

•http://degreeforum.net

•Instacert.com

Other resources

- Comex books - specific for each CLEP

- free-clep-prep.com - a new website with free CLEP and Dantes study resources

Types of Tests

- CLEP

- DANTES

- Excelsior - only if you really need to - hard and $

TECEP - These are specifically Thomas Edison State

College tests

About Kathy Cooksey:

Kathy Cooksey is a mom of 8 children from 3 to 21 years old.

Her husband Ronny is the pastor of a church in McMinnville, Oregon. After graduating with her Bachelor of Arts in Elementary Education with Math Specialization, Kathy enjoyed being an Admissions Counselor at Dallas Baptist University and then taught 1st grade to some delightful students in Texas.

When her oldest, Micah, was 3 years old and the family lived in Japan as Southern Baptist missionaries, she started her own school — at the kitchen table. She has homeschooled all her children since then. When Kathy is not spending time with her children (and sometimes when she is!), she enjoys singing, reading, gardening, researching politics, and visiting the gorgeous Oregon Coast.

Because of God's grace, her son Micah finished his B.A. by the age of 16, and now has a Master's degree as well.

Made in the USA
San Bernardino, CA
31 July 2014